Rain

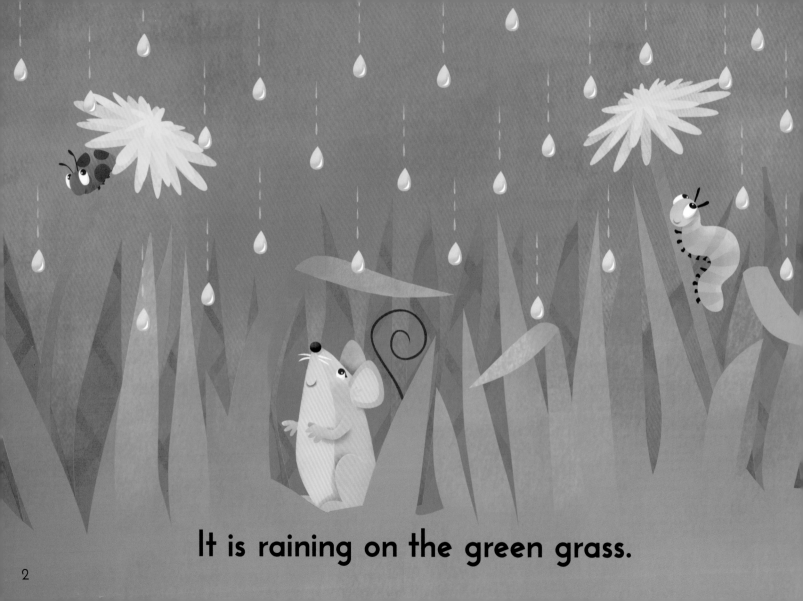

It is raining on the green grass.

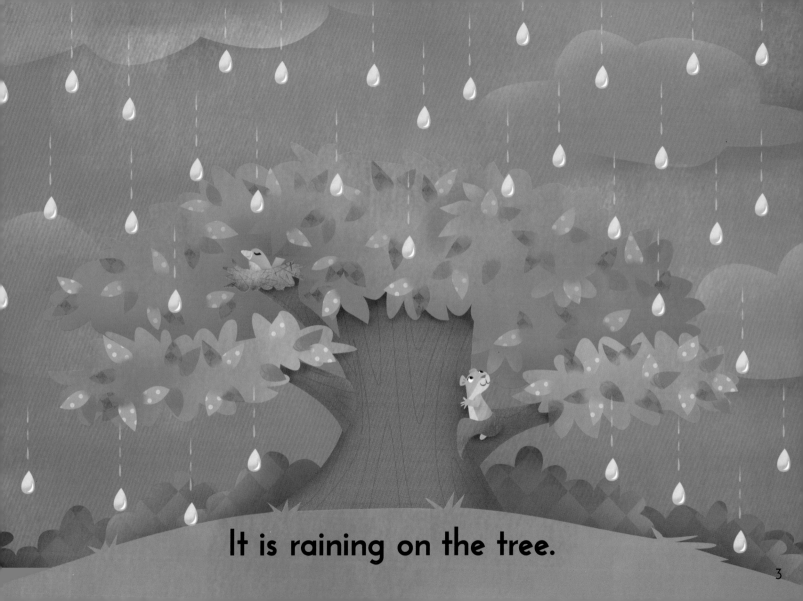

It is raining on the tree.

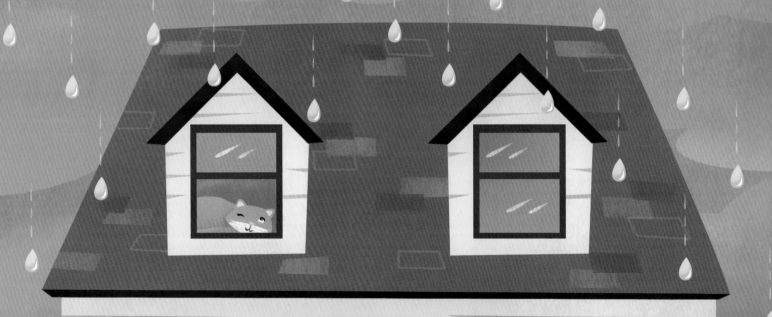

It is raining on the rooftop,

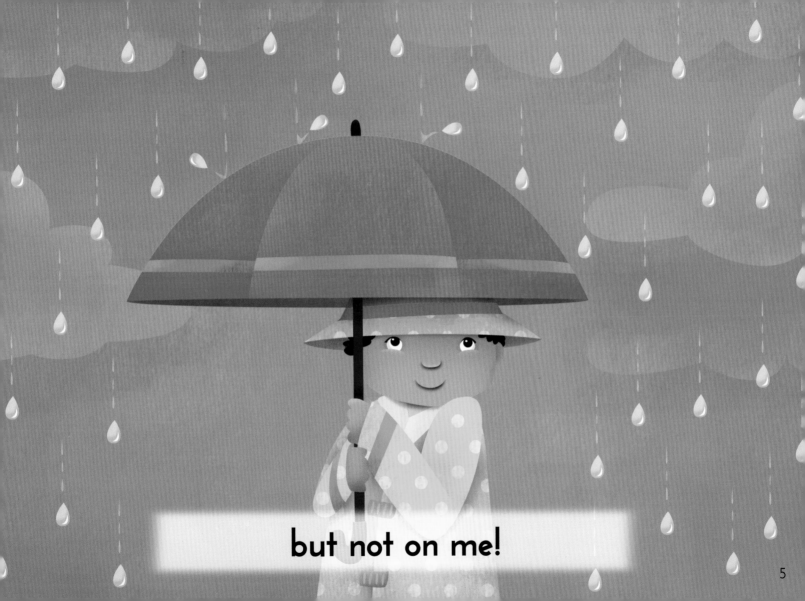

but not on me!

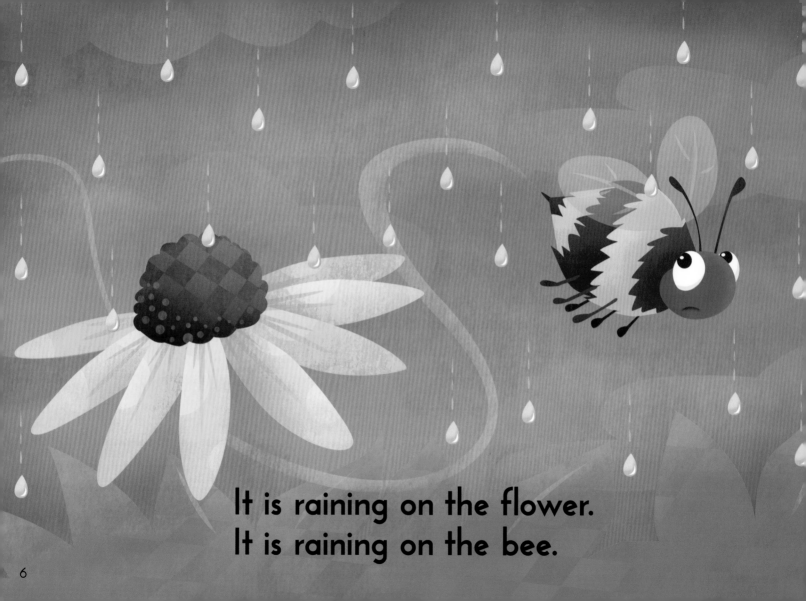

It is raining on the flower.
It is raining on the bee.

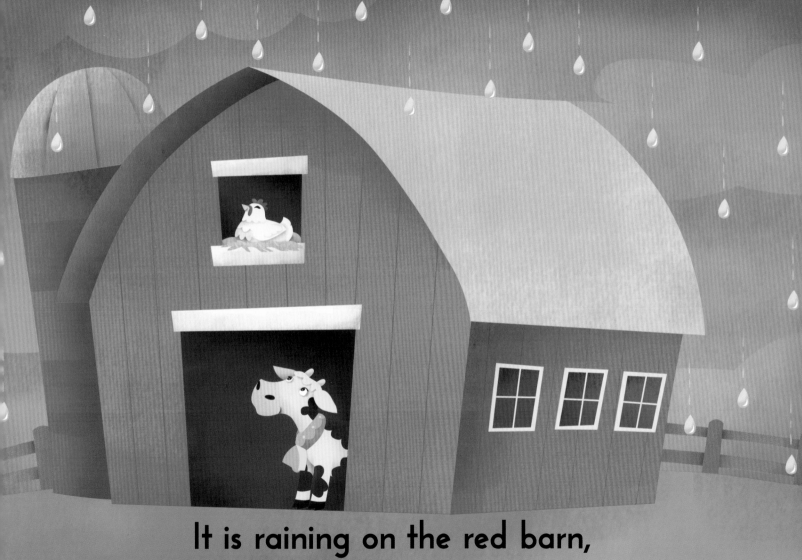

It is raining on the red barn,

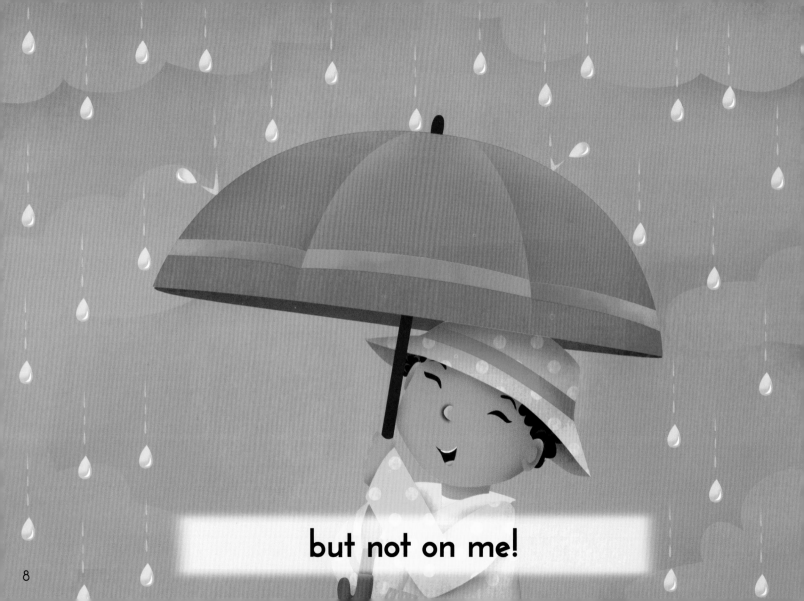

but not on me!